Life Cycles

by Sascha Goddard

OXFORD

UNIVERSITY PRESS

AUSTRALIA & NEW ZEALAND

Patterns of Life

Life goes around in a **cycle**. Baby animals are born, then they grow and change. Some animals **transform** as they grow, others just grow bigger.

When animals become adults, they have their own **young**. This is called a life cycle.

Some animals lay eggs that hatch and others have live young.

Not all life cycles are the same. But they all follow the same pattern, which keeps going around and around in a circle.

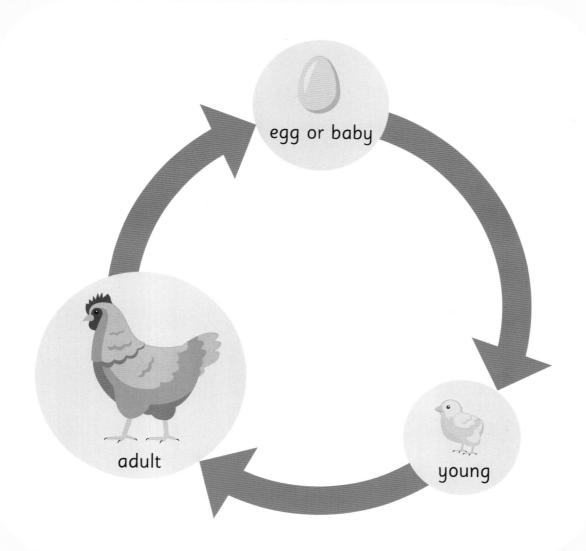

egg or baby

young

adult

Living the Snail Life

Hatching out

The life of a snail begins with an egg.

When snail eggs hatch, tiny snails with soft shells **emerge**.

To break out of the shell, a snail uses its radula, which is like a row of sharp teeth.

Slowly and carefully, the snails explore their world.
They need to find food.

Growing up

As time passes, snails grow bigger.
Their spiral-shaped shells grow with them.

In around one year, a snail will be fully **mature**.

Snail shells become harder as they grow.

Body protection

A snail's shell protects it from **predators**. It also keeps the snail moist and protects it from hot and dry weather. Snails can pull their whole bodies back into their shells.

Laying eggs

Both male and female snails can lay eggs. They lay them in damp holes in the soil.

The eggs will hatch in two to four weeks, but they will not all survive. Some will dry out and die, others will be eaten by predators.

Fun fact

Snails can lay 80 eggs or more at a time.

Most snails live for about two to seven years.

Life cycle of a snail

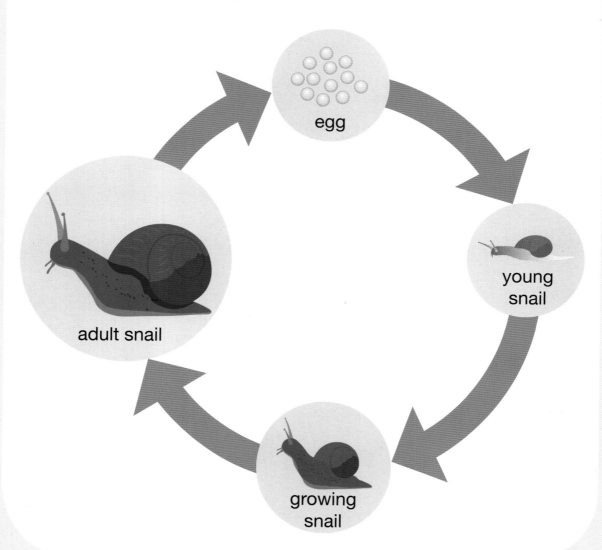

egg

young
snail

growing
snail

adult snail

The Life of a Hedgehog

A live birth

Hedgehogs give birth to live young called hoglets. Their short, soft spines come out soon after they are born.

Hedgehogs can have four or five hoglets at a time.

Hoglets have to learn to survive on their own.

The mother hedgehog takes care of the little hoglets.
For the first few weeks, the hoglets stay in the nest.
When they are ready, the mother hedgehog shows
them how to find food.

Growing hoglets

When hedgehogs are about four to six weeks old, they leave their mother and become **independent**.

Young hedgehogs need as much food as possible. Getting bigger will give them a better chance of surviving the winter.

Hedgehogs eat insects, snails, eggs and more.

Body protection

By this time, hedgehogs have hard, long, sharp spines. Spines cover most of a hedgehog's body. When in danger, a hedgehog will stick out its sharp spines and roll into a ball. This protects it from predators.

Fun fact

A fully grown hedgehog can have more than 5000 spines!

New hoglets

When they are about two years old, hedgehogs can have their own hoglets.

Female hedgehogs give birth to hoglets in late summer or autumn.

Hedgehogs can live for around seven years.

Life cycle of a hedgehog

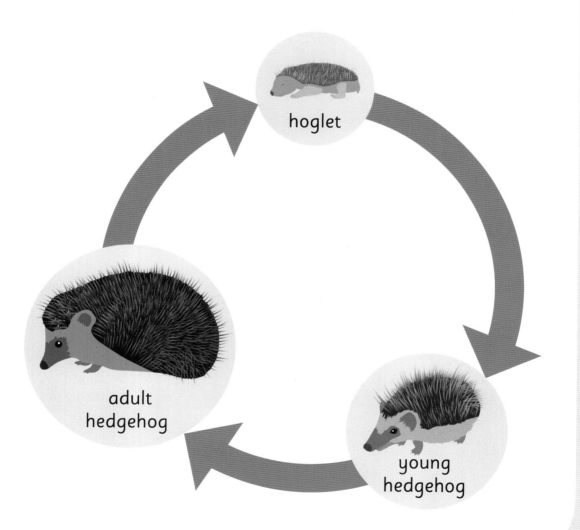

hoglet

young
hedgehog

adult
hedgehog

A Blue Crab's Life

First comes the egg

Blue crabs hatch from eggs that are carried on a female crab's body. The tiny creatures emerge and drift away in the water.

Millions of blue crab eggs hatch at the same time.

The tiny blue crab is smaller than an ant.

At first, they don't look like crabs. The creatures are see-through and have no legs or shell.

The tiny crabs float on top of the sea. The water must be clean, warm enough and have plenty of air in it, or many of the tiny crabs will not survive.

Changing as they grow

Slowly the blue crab transforms, changing its shape many times. Finally, it becomes a young crab.

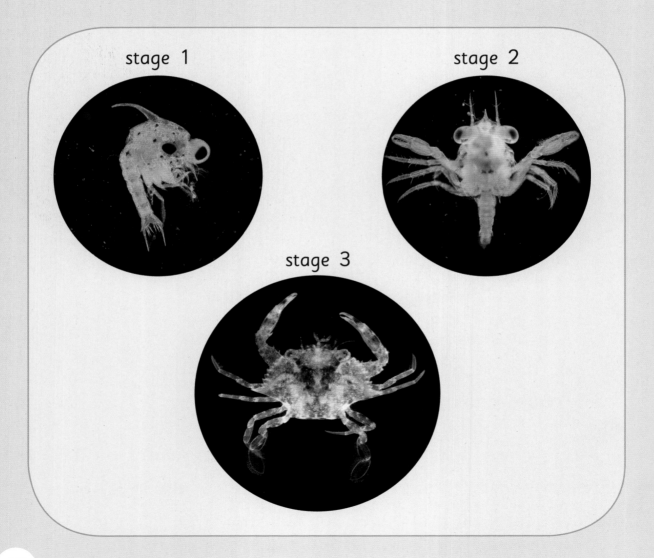

stage 1

stage 2

stage 3

Body protection

The young blue crab has a skeleton on the outside of its body. This is called an **exoskeleton**, or shell.

As the crab grows, it sheds its exoskeleton about 20 times, growing a bigger one each time. After more than a year, it becomes a fully grown blue crab. The male adult is called a jimmy and the female is called a sook.

The hard exoskeleton of an adult crab provides great protection. The tough shell makes it very hard for predators to get to the body of a crab.

Its exoskeleton will help a crab survive an attack.

A sponge full of eggs

When a sook has shed her shell for the last time, she is ready to lay eggs.

The sook carries her eggs on the outside of her body. The enormous group of eggs is called a sponge.

About two weeks later, the eggs hatch. The tiny, strange-looking creatures drift away from the sook, into the sea.

Fun fact

The bright orange sponge of a blue crab can contain up to 2 million eggs!

sponge

Life cycle of a blue crab

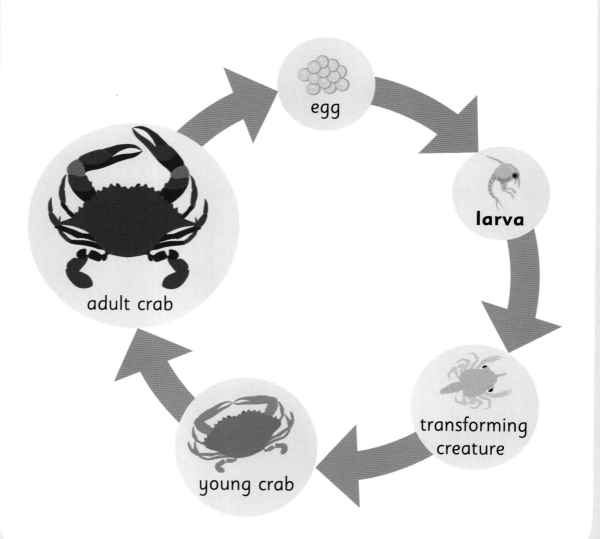

egg

larva

transforming creature

young crab

adult crab

Comparing Life Cycles

Animal	Snail	Hedgehog	Blue crab
How is it born?	hatching egg	live birth	hatching egg
Does its body transform?	no	no	yes
What protects its body?	shell	spines	exoskeleton
How long does it live?	two to seven years	around seven years	one to three years

Glossary

cycle: a process that follows a circular pattern

emerge: come out of

independent: can look after itself

larva: a stage after coming out of an egg

mature: fully grown

predators: animals that hunt and eat other animals

transform: change shape

young: baby animals, or animals that are still growing

Index